Duck-billed Platypus

Illustrations: Janet Moneymaker
Design/Editing: Marjie Bassler

Copyright © 2023 by Rebecca Woodbury, Ph.D.

All rights reserved. No part of this publication may be reproduced, stored in a retrieval system, or transmitted, in any form or by any means, electronic, mechanical, photocopying, recording, or otherwise, without prior written permission from the publisher. No part of this book may be reproduced in any manner whatsoever without written permission.

Duck-billed Platypus
ISBN 978-1-950415-69-4

Published by Gravitas Publications Inc.
Imprint: Real Science-4-Kids
www.gravitaspublications.com
www.realscience4kids.com

The duck-billed **platypus** is a very odd animal.

A platypus has a bill like a duck, lays eggs like a duck, and has webbed feet.

Does that make it a duck?

Yes. It must be a kind of duck.

A platypus has a flat tail like a beaver and fur like a beaver.

Does that make it a beaver?

Hmm. Is it a duck-beaver?

A platypus is like a duck in some ways and also like a beaver. But the platypus belongs to a different group of animals called **monotremes**. **Platypuses** and **echnidas** are the only monotremes.

Oh. A platypus is NOT a kind of duck or a kind of beaver.

Most mammals give birth to live babies. Monotremes are mammals that lay **eggs**.

Mice are mammals.

WHAT ARE MAMMALS

Mammals are animals that have some things in common. They:

- Breathe air
- Feed milk to their babies
- Have fur for at least part of their life.
- Most mammals give birth to live babies.
- **Monotremes** are the only mammals that lay eggs. There are only two types of monotremes.

Platypuses live by lakes and slow-moving rivers.

They eat when they are in water, most often at night. Their food includes bugs, beetles, shrimps, snails, and worms.

Ick! Bugs!

The platypus uses its bill to snap up food from the water. It also eats by using its bill to look for food at the bottom of rivers and lakes.

Platypuses sleep in burrows near the edge of rivers and lakes.

"Looks cozy."

A female platypus lays 1-3 eggs and takes care of the babies when the eggs hatch.

The male platypus has a sharp spur on each of its hind legs. The spur can release a poison.

The platypus is found only in **Australia**.

There is much more to learn about his surprising animal.

Australia

The red areas show where platypuses live.
Illustration by Tentotwo, CC BY SA 3.0

How to say science words

Australia   (aw-STRAYL-yuh)

echidna   (i-KID-nuh)

egg   (AIG)

mammal   (MAA-muhl)

monotreme   (MAH-nuh-treem)

platypus   (PLAA-ti-puhs)

science   (SIY-uhns)

What questions do you have about PLATYPUSES?

Learn More Real Science!

Complete science curricula from Real Science-4-Kids

Focus On Series

Unit study for elementary and middle school levels

Chemistry
Biology
Physics
Geology
Astronomy

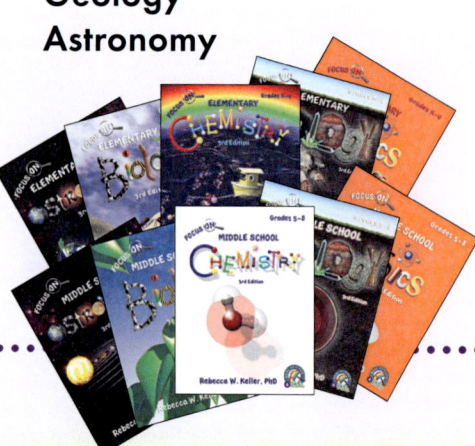

Exploring Science Series

Graded series for levels K–8. Each book contains 4 chapters of:

Chemistry
Biology
Physics
Geology
Astronomy

Printed by BoD in Norderstedt, Germany